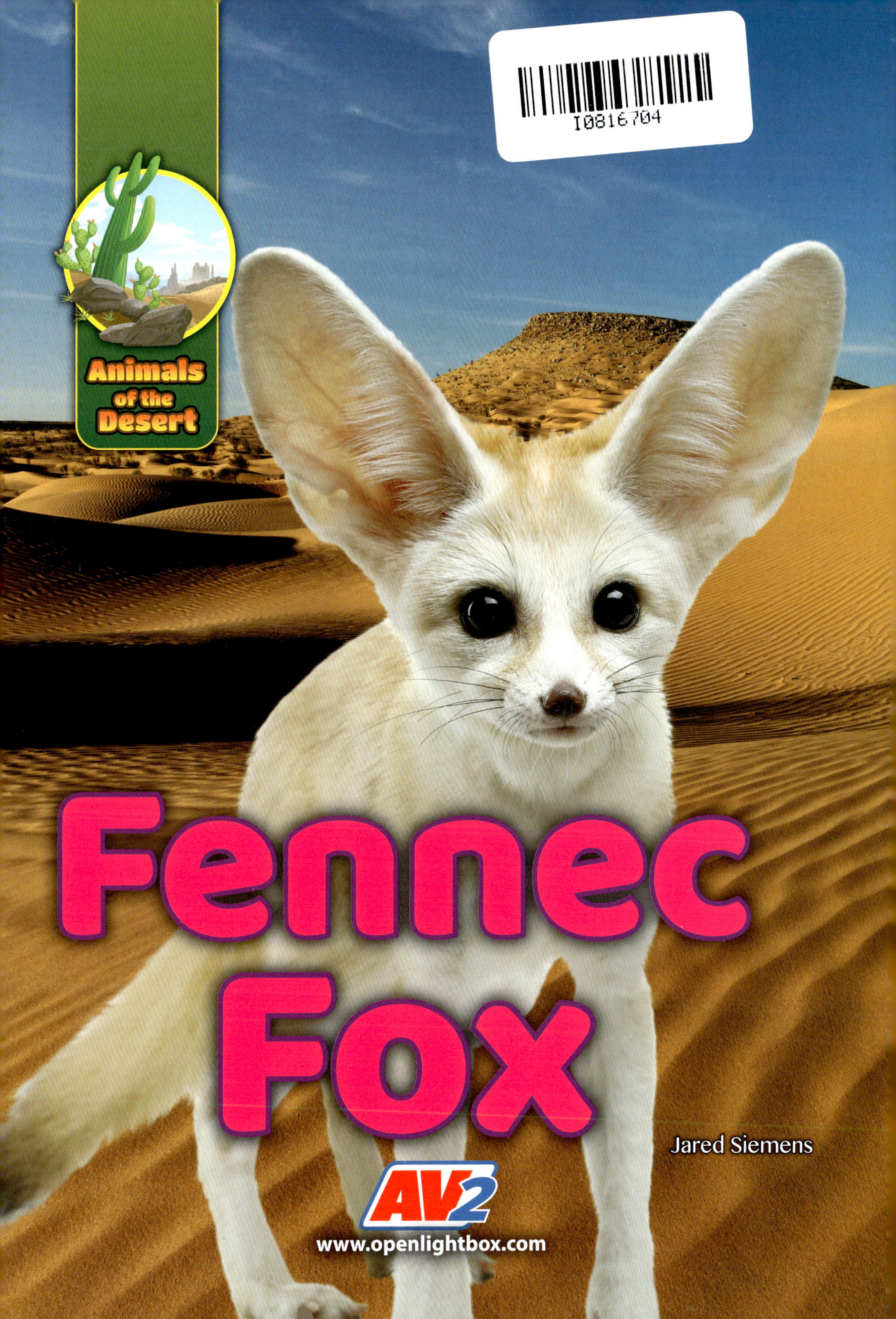
Animals of the Desert
Fennec Fox
Jared Siemens
AV2
www.openlightbox.com

Step 1
Go to **www.openlightbox.com**

Step 2
Enter this unique code
XOAWD0KG4

Step 3
Explore your interactive eBook!

AV2 is optimized for use on any device

Your interactive eBook comes with...

Contents
Browse a live contents page to easily navigate through resources

Audio
Listen to sections of the book read aloud

Videos
Watch informative video clips

Weblinks
Gain additional information for research

Slideshows
View images and captions

Try This!
Complete activities and hands-on experiments

Key Words
Study vocabulary, and complete a matching word activity

Quizzes
Test your knowledge

Share
Share titles within your Learning Management System (LMS) or Library Circulation System

Citation
Create bibliographical references following APA, CMOS, and MLA styles

This title is part of our AV2 digital subscription

1-Year Grades K–5 Subscription
ISBN 978-1-7911-3320-7

Access hundreds of AV2 titles with our digital subscription.
Sign up for a FREE trial at **www.openlightbox.com/trial**

Fennec Fox

CONTENTS

Meet the Fennec Fox

The fennec fox is known mostly for its small **stature** and large ears. Fennec foxes are often called "desert foxes" because they live in desert and semi-desert areas of North Africa. The English word "fennec" comes from the Arabic word *fanak*, which means "fox."

Tiny Foxes

A fennec fox stands about 7.1 to 8.6 inches (18 to 22 centimeters) tall at the shoulder. This makes it the smallest member of the Canidae family of **mammals**. Along with foxes, Canidae includes dogs and wolves.

Fennec foxes are also very light. Adults weigh between 2.2 and 3.3 pounds (1 and 1.5 kilograms). This is roughly the same weight as a 3-month-old kitten.

Height Difference

FENNEC FOX
8.6 inches
(22 cm)

ARCTIC FOX
12 inches
(30 cm)

RED FOX
15 inches
(38 cm)

Fox Families

Fennec foxes live in groups of up to 10. Groups of fennec foxes are called skulks. Skulks typically include family units of a mother, a father, and their offspring.

Skulks often make their homes in underground burrows. These can be 3 feet (1 meter) deep and up to 32 feet (10 m) long. Sometimes, multiple fennec fox families will share a large burrow.

Fennec foxes communicate using many different sounds. These include barks, growls, and shrieks.

Comparing Average Life Spans
Red Fox
3
years
Arctic Fox
4
years
Fennec Fox
10
years

Growing Up

Once a year, during their **breeding season**, female fennec foxes will have a single **litter.** Young fennec foxes are known as kits. Fennec foxes are born with their eyes closed.

The kits grow quickly. They can see after their first week, and can walk at two weeks of age. Fennec foxes are considered adults when they are 6 to 11 months old.

FOX FACT

A fennec fox can have up to **six kits** in a litter.

A Closer Look

Fennec foxes have **adapted** to their **habitats**. They have unique features that help them survive in their environment.

Fur

A fennec fox's sandy-colored fur **reflects** light during the day, helping the fox keep cool. The fur also helps it stay warm at night.

Legs

Despite its small size, a fennec fox can run at speeds up to 25 miles (40 kilometers) per hour.

Eyes

The eyes of a fennec fox reflect light. This helps the animal see more easily at night.

Claws

A fennec fox's feet have curved claws that are excellent for digging.

Feet

A fennec fox has fur on the bottom of its feet. This helps protect its feet from hot or cold desert sands.

Keeping Cool

Fennec foxes are nocturnal, which means they are most active at night. By sleeping underground during the day, they avoid the scorching heat of the desert sunlight. This also helps them avoid **predators**, such as birds, that are active during the day.

If fennec foxes become too hot, they can cool down quickly by panting. When temperatures exceed 95° Fahrenheit (35° Celsius), they may take up to 690 breaths a minute.

Fennec fox burrows typically have multiple entrances. This makes it easier for the foxes to flee from danger.

15

Exceptional Ears

The fennec fox's 6-inch (15-cm)-long ears provide it with strong hearing. The ear's size and shape help the fennec fox hear the insects it eats as they walk along the surface of the sand or under the ground. Another important **function** of a fennec fox's ears is to cool the fox by releasing **excess** body heat.

FOX FACT

Fennec foxes have the largest **ears** compared to body size of any member of the **Canidae family**.

Fennec Fox

Finding Food

Fennec foxes are omnivorous. They eat both plants and animals. Although they live in groups, they hunt on their own. Each night, fennec foxes use their extraordinary hearing to find **prey** under the sand. Then, they use their claws to dig it up. Fennec foxes also like to eat fruit, roots, and eggs. These foxes are able to survive without drinking water. Instead, they get most of the water they need from their food.

Fennec foxes hunt a wide range of prey. This includes insects, rodents, and lizards.

Fennec Foxes in Danger

Fennec foxes are not considered to be **endangered**. They are found throughout the Sahara Desert. However, populations in some areas do face threats. **Encroaching** human settlements have caused fennec foxes to lose their habitat in some areas of Morocco. Due to their unique appearance, fennec foxes are targets for the pet trade. They may also be hunted for their fur.

Fennec foxes are protected by law in Algeria, Egypt, Morocco, and Tunisia.

Fox Conservation Status

Extinct

Extinct in the Wild

Critically Endangered

Endangered

Vulnerable

Near Threatened

Least Concern

Fennec Fox

Red Fox

Arctic Fox

Fennec Fox Quiz

1 Where do fennec foxes get most of their water?

2 How does a fennec fox's fur help keep it cool during the day?

3 How many fennec foxes can be in a group?

4 Where are fennec foxes protected by law?

5 When are fennec foxes most active?

6 How many fennec fox kits can be in a litter?

7 Why do fennec fox burrows have multiple entrances?

8 How long can a fennec fox live?

ANSWERS **1.** From their food **2.** By reflecting light **3.** Up to 10 **4.** In Algeria, Egypt, Morocco, and Tunisia **5.** At night **6.** Up to six **7.** To make it easier for the foxes to flee from danger **8.** About 10 years

Key Words

adapted: changed to suit the environment

breeding season: a time during which animals reproduce

encroaching: slowly and steadily invading

endangered: in danger of no longer existing in the world

excess: more than needed

function: the purpose for which something is used

habitats: the places where animals live, grow, and raise their young

litter: a group of animals born at the same time

mammals: warm-blooded animals that have hair or fur and nurse their young

predators: animals that live by killing other animals for food

prey: animals eaten by others as food

reflects: bounces something back toward its source

stature: natural height

Index

Get the best of both worlds.

AV2 bridges the gap between print and digital.

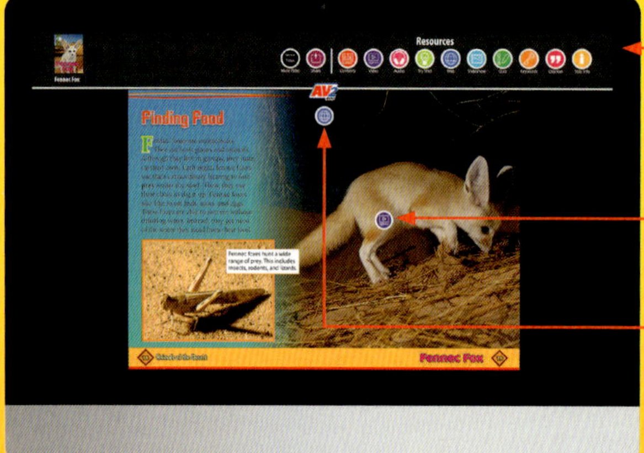

The expandable resources toolbar enables quick access to content including **videos**, **audio**, **activities**, **weblinks**, **slideshows**, **quizzes**, and **key words**.

Animated videos make static images come alive.

Resource icons on each page help readers to further **explore key concepts**.

Published by Lightbox Learning Inc.
276 5th Avenue, Suite 704 #917
New York, NY 10001
Website: www.openlightbox.com

Library of Congress Control Number: 2022947461

ISBN 978-1-7911-4790-7 (hardcover)
ISBN 978-1-7911-4791-4 (softcover)
ISBN 978-1-7911-4792-1 (multi-user eBook)

Printed in Guangzhou, China
1 2 3 4 5 6 7 8 9 0 26 25 24 23 22

102022
101121

Layout: Sushant Deshpande Project Coordinator: John Willis

Every reasonable effort has been made to trace ownership and to obtain permission to reprint copyright material. The publisher would be pleased to have any errors or omissions brought to its attention so that they may be corrected in subsequent printings.

The publisher acknowledges Alamy, Dreamstime, Getty Images, Minden Pictures, and Shutterstock as the primary image suppliers for this title.